Trust God No Matter What!

The Biblical Way To Handle Trials

Proverbs 3:5-6

John T. Cocoris, Th.M., M.A., Psy.D.

Trust God No Matter What!
The Biblical Way To Handle Trials

© Temperament Dynamics, LLC
4848 Lemmon Ave.
STE 152
Dallas, TX 75219

www.discstrengths.com
info@discstrengths.com
512-553-8104

Library of Congress Card Number:
ISBN: 978-1-948474-06-1
12-23-25

Temperament Dynamics, LLC
Dallas, Texas 75219

Cover design and interior design and layout by
John T. Cocoris

Printed in the United States of America

Table of Contents

Table of Contents

Preface

Why this book? This book was written to give you hope that God is with you no matter what you are going through. God wants you to Trust Him no matter what that is!

I became a Christian when I was in high school. Soon after I became a believer I decided that I was unskilled in how to live life. Really, I was not prepared to enter adulthood. One afternoon while pondering what I was going to do with my life I ask God to give me wisdom. Little did I know what lay ahead.

In order to learn God's wisdom I had to go through storms in my life. In the trials I often responded with anxiety, fear, anger, and depression. I did not always respond Biblically. God was patient and gracious with me throughout my struggles. Learning to "Trust God no matter what!" is not easy nor does it happen quickly. It takes time for God to prove to you that He will always be there for you and with you.

I've gone through significant trials over the course of my life and recently, the most challenging of all. The situation was life changing and clear to me and my wife that a favorable outcome looked impossible. The situation drove me to search the Scripture for comfort and guidance. This book is the result of that study.

It is my desire that you will embrace the Scriptures that God has provided to give you guidance, comfort, and hope no matter what you are going through. Learn to think Biblically and learn to trust God...no matter what!

Author's Note: Some of the material in this book is from another book I wrote, *3 Reasons Why Christians Go To Counseling*, 2015.

In the world ye shall have tribulation:
but be of good cheer;
I have overcome the world.

John 16:33

Chapter 1

Proverbs 3:5-6

Trust in the Lord with all your heart, And lean not on your own understanding; 6 In all your ways acknowledge Him, And He shall direct your paths.

What ever else you learn to do in this life learn to trust God no matter what happens. To say it is hard to trust God in all the difficulties you encounter is an understatement...I know.

As we will see, the ultimate goal of living the spiritual life is to become like Jesus Christ (Romans 8:28-29). To accomplish this goal you have to trust that God knows what He is doing in your life with the trials you encounter. God knows what you need, when you need it, and how much you need. He uses everything that happens in your life and He is using what you are currently going through.

As a young believer, I took Proverbs 3:5-6 as my life's verse not realizing just how important it would become. It was through this verse that I learned that it's best to trust God no matter what.

Without trials in your life you cannot grow spiritually and become like Christ. Let's take a closer look at Proverbs 3:5-6.

The Hebrew word for "Trust" *means to have confidence in, to feel safe*. So when you *trust in the Lord* you can feel confident and safe in doing so. But we are to trust "with all your heart" which includes your mind, emotions, and will.

We are told to *lean not on your own understanding.* Notice the contrast is between trusting the Lord and trusting your own understanding. If we trust the Lord, we cannot *also* depend upon our ability to understand what God is doing. We naturally have a need to make sense out of what is going on in our lives.

Sumner Wemp, my spiritual grandfather, said to me, that Proverbs 3:5-6 is teaching us *don't try to figure it out.* Just trust that the Lord knows what He is doing.

Do not forget that it is God Who is directing your life. It is God Who determines what is best for you. It is God Who has the final decision. Not you nor I. It is God Who sees the whole picture while we see only a tiny piece. Someone put it this way;

> To trust in the Lord with all our heart means we can't place **our** own **right** to understand above **His right** to direct our lives the way He sees fit. When we insist on God always making sense to our finite minds, we are setting ourselves up for spiritual trouble. (Author unknown)

We are told, *In all your ways acknowledge Him, And He shall direct your paths.* Now, the benefit, when you trust Him with all your heart, is that He will direct you.

My brother, Mike, (author and pastor), wrote this comment on Proverbs 3:5-6:

The Hebrew word for "direct" means "smooth, straight, right." Smooth is being free from obstacles. These verses are not promising daily direction in all the decisions we make. They are saying that if we follow the Lord, He will make our lives go straight in the sense of righteousness, smooth in the sense of removing all hindrances out of the way.

Biblical Thinking
Trust God no matter what.

PART I

WHY DO WE HAVE TRIALS?

Chapter 2

Nine Reasons For Trials & Suffering

Ever wonder why there is so much suffering in this world? Ever ask "Why me, why now, why this?"

There are at least nine reasons for suffering mentioned in the Bible. Here is a brief overview:

1. **Adam's sin.**
   Due to Adam's sin we have physical diseases. Jesus healed many who were sick, including the blind, lepers, one with a skin disease, those paralyzed, and more.

2. **Satan's attack; Job 1:6-12.**
   God allowed satan to test Job and he suffered greatly.

3. **Consequences of sin; Gal. 6:7-8.**
   Do not be deceived, God is not mocked; for whatever a man sows, that he will also reap. 8 For he who sows to his flesh will of the flesh reap corruption, but he who sows to the Spirit will of the Spirit reap everlasting life.

4. **Call to salvation; John 4:46-54.**
   Sometimes God will use an illness to get someone saved. In this passage not only was the nobleman saved but everyone in his family.

5. Life-style differs from the world; II Tim 3:12.

All that live Godly in Christ Jesus shall suffer persecution. We are currently experiencing attacks on Christianity and Christians like never before in the history of the United States.

6. Chastisement or character training; Heb. 12:5-6.

My son, do not despise the chastening of the Lord, Nor be discouraged when you are rebuked by Him; 6 For whom the Lord loves He chastens, and scourges every son whom He receives.

7. For the glory of God, John 9:1-3.

Now as Jesus passed by, He saw a man who was blind from birth. 2 And His disciples asked Him, saying, "Rabbi, who sinned, this man or his parents, that he was born blind?" 3 Jesus answered, "Neither this man nor his parents sinned, but that the works of God should be revealed in him.

8. Conformity to Christ; Romans 8:28-29:

And we know that all things work together for good to those who love God, to those who are the called according to His purpose. 29 For whom He foreknew, He also predestined to be conformed to the image of His Son, that He might be the firstborn among many brethern.

All suffering is *used* to conform us into the likeness of Christ. Please note this passage does not say God *causes* all things, it teaches that God *uses* all things.

The following three things happened to Jesus while in the Garden of Gethsemane just before His crucifixion:

A. **Betrayed**. Jesus was betrayed by Judas; Matthew 26:48-49:

Now His betrayer had given them a sign, saying, "Whomever I kiss, He is the One; seize Him." 49 Immediately he went up to Jesus and said, "Greetings, Rabbi!" and kissed Him.

B. **Abandoned**. Jesus was abandoned by the rest of the disciples; Matthew 26:55-56:

In that hour Jesus said to the multitudes, "Have you come out, as against a robber, with swords and clubs to take Me? I sat daily with you, teaching in the temple, and you did not seize Me. 56 But all this was done that the Scriptures of the prophets might be fulfilled." Then all the disciples forsook Him and fled.

C. **Denied**. Jesus was denied by Peter; Matthew 26:69-70:

Now Peter sat outside in the courtyard. And a servant girl came to him, saying, "You also were with Jesus of Galilee." 70 But he denied it before them all, saying, "I do not know what you are saying."

9. **To be able to comfort others; II Corinthians 1:3-4**:
Blessed be the God and Father of our Lord Jesus Christ, the Father of mercies and God of all comfort, 4 who comforts us in all our tribulation, that we may be able to comfort we those who are in any trouble, with the comfort with which ourselves are comforted by God.

Biblical Thinking

There are many reasons why suffering happens in this world and in the life of a believer.

God will use your response to trials to help you grow spiritually and to comfort others that are going through difficulties.

Suffering is temporary (Rev. 21:4):

And God will wipe away every tear from their eyes; there shall be no more death, nor sorrow, nor crying. There shall be no more pain, for the former things have passed away.

Chuck Swindoll

"We're all faced with a series of great opportunities brilliantly disguised as impossible situations."

PART II

THE PURPOSE OF TRIALS

Life is what happens while you'er
busy making other plans!
Allen Saunders, 1957

Chapter 3

Do Not Be Surprised

1 Peter 4:12

Beloved, do not think it strange concerning the fiery trial which is to try you, as though some strange thing happened to you;

You can be blind sided, surprised, and overwhelmed when pain and suffering come rushing into your life. Some Christians believe and expect that they should be spared trouble and pain (big or small). Still others get angry at God blaming Him for their circumstances. These responses could not be further from what the Bible teaches. We should not be surprised or angry because Jesus told us clearly that tribulation (trials, trouble, storms) and life are inseparable.

John 16:33

*These things I have spoken to you, that in Me you may have peace. In the world you will have **tribulation**; but be of good cheer, I have overcome the world.*

The Greek word for *tribulation* means *pressing or pressure or anything that burdens the spirit*. It can be translated *anguish, burdened, persecution, tribulation,* or *trouble*. This passage is

13

teaching us to not be *surprised* or *shocked* when life's trouble happens.

As both a pastor and professional counselor I have spoken to a large number of Christians over the years that were going through a difficult time in their lives and did not understand why. Everyone came to me surprised and feeling overwhelmed. Many would say, "Why is this happening to me?" Many believed that God was mad at them or He was punishing them for something they had done.

The first thing you need to understand is that God uses trials or suffering for a purpose.

The second thing you need to understand is we Christians normally think of trials as something happening to us, that we are innocent of blame. However, sometimes we cause trouble by making bad choices. Does that mean the promises of God are not available because you caused the trouble? No! All of God's promises to help are for all of us regardless of fault!

As you will see, God is doing something in your life through whatever you are experiencing. Learn to trust Him no matter what because He knows what He's doing.

Biblical Thinking

Do not be surprised when trials happen because they are a part of living and growing in the Spiritual life. Trust God no matter what!

Chapter 4

All Things Work Together For Good

Romans 8:28-29

And we know that all things work together for good to those who love God, to those who are the called according to His purpose. 29 For whom He foreknew, He also predestined to be conformed to the image of His Son, that He might be the firstborn among many brethren.

As a Christian, there are two ways to look at your life events. You are either a *victim* of circumstances or there is *divine purpose* behind the events of your life.

God's divine purpose for all life's events is in Romans 8:28-29. It states that "all things work together for good." It does not say some, many, or most "things work together" but "all things." The accident, the lost relationship, the failed marriage, the rebellious child, the lost job, illness, financial crisis, loosing your favorite pen, the fire, being betrayed by a family member or friend, etc.

I cannot possible mentioned everything someone may go through in life but you get the idea. All things, yes everything that happens in your life, will be *used* by God to help conform you into the image of His Son, no exceptions! This means that...

God doesn't do anything TO you,
He allows it FOR you.

Notice also that the passage does not say that *all things are good*. It says that *all things* are being **used for good**. The greek word for *good* includes in the definition the idea of *benefit*. So all the events in your life have **benefit** in conforming you into the image of His Son.

Of course, you may not see the *benefit* when you are in the event. You can only have faith that God will somehow use the event to accomplish the goal of conforming you into the likeness of His Son.

Actually, this is what it means to walk by faith; you may not see how the event will be *beneficial* but God does. Trust God that He knows what He is doing in your current circumstance.

Here is what my brother, Mike, wrote in, *The Spiritual Life, Clarifying The Confusion* about being conformed into the image of Christ:, page 23, 2024.

Let's review, thus far, I have described the nature of the spiritual life as a process of growing to Christ-like maturity in the context of a spiritual community. In other words, the goal of the spiritual life is Christ-like maturity.

The question becomes, "What is Christ-like maturity?" Being God, Christ is holy and love. When He walked on this earth as a human, He was full of grace and truth. He was meek and gentle. He was submissive and had a servant's heart.

That is only the beginning. The New Testament contains several lists of virtues believers need to develop (Gal. 5:22-23; 2 Cor. 6:4-10; 1 Tim. 6:11; Rev. 2:19). The items in these lists are characteristics of Christ-like maturity. Second Peter 1:5-7 is one of those lists that should be carefully considered.

Dr. Tom Constable, in his notes on Romans 8:28-29, puts it this way:

His aim for them [Christians] now is not to make them happy, materially prosperous, or famous, but to make them Christlike. He now uses 'all things,' the sad as well as the glad, the painful as well as the pleasant, the things that perplex and disappoint as well as the things they eagerly strive and pray for, to further His eternal purpose for them. In His infinite wisdom He knows what is needed to bring about that transformation. For some of His own He may need to use hotter fire and strike with harder blows than in His dealings with others to effect the formation of Christ's image in them. This may be because some believers may be more resistant to His moulding activities or are more prone to insist on their own efforts.

God's chosen method to conform us into His image is pain and suffering through trials. It is only in our pain and suffering that we learn of God's mercy, grace, provision, and peace. It is only in our pain and suffering that we learn to know Him and to depend upon Him.

A walk by the river:

A man was casually walking down a small path on the river bank when he noticed a man standing at the end of a pier. He stopped to observe what he was doing. It was a bit puzzling to the traveler because he appeared to be separating logs as they were floating down the river. He had a long pole with a hook on the end and was using it to push some of the logs out into the main stream and others he would pull into a small cove next to the pier. His actions seemed to be random and without purpose.

His curiosity drove him to ask the man just what he was up to. He walked out on the pier and said, "Excuse me sir but what exactly are you doing?" The older gentleman paused and said, "Well, some of the logs are good for building houses so I'm pushing them out into the main stream so they will be carried to the mill." "What about the other ones" he asked?

The worker replied, "Well those are only good for making toothpicks, so I'm separating them to the side." Now the traveler's curiosity was even greater and he asked the obvious question, "And just how do you know the difference?"

The old worker look at him and said, "When you've done this as long as I have you can tell which trees were raised on the mountain tops and which ones were raise in the valley."

He then explained that, "The ones that were raised in the valley are not much good because they have not been exposed to the wind and they are not strong enough to be used for houses. They could only be used for toothpicks. Now the ones that were raised on the top of the mountain were subjected to the strong winds and were made strong enough to be used to build houses."

18

The only way to grow to maturity is to experience the punishing winds of life. If however, you ignore the lessons from the winds and storms of life you will not grow spiritually nor will you be useful to God.

Paul did what he taught

Someone said a long time ago, "Don't do as I do, Do as I say do!" It wasn't the Apostle Paul. He lived what he taught.

It appears that Paul wrote Romans in February, 57 A.D. He then wrote II Corinthians in March, 57 A.D. only a month later.

He believed that all things work together for good, Romans 8:28-29. He believed that regardless of what happened in his life he *trusted God*! II Corinthians 1:8-11:

For we do not want you to be ignorant, brethren, of our trouble which came to us in Asia: that we were burdened beyond measure, above strength, so that we despaired even of life. 9 Yes, we had the sentence of death in ourselves, that we should not trust in ourselves but in God who raises the dead, 10 who delivered us from so great a death, and does deliver us; in whom we trust that He will still deliver us, 11 you also helping together in prayer for us, that thanks may be given by many persons on our behalf for the gift granted to us through many.

Paul did not reveal exactly what was happening in his life that caused him to pen these words. He wrote this to express the intensity of the events (Constable). What we gain from his experience is that it happened so that he would trust God no matter what was

19

going on! It was so bad that he thought he was going to die!

Ever felt like that? Yeah, me too. Paul's conclusion was that it happened so he would not trust in himself, but trust in God! Why trust God? He identifies God as the one who raises the dead! Why did he say that? Well, if God can raise the dead He can deliever me even if I'm about to die!

He did deliever Paul. And He can deliever you regardless of what you're going through right now. Who is more powerful than One Who can raise the dead? Trust God no matter what!

Biblical Thinking

Everything that happens in your life is designed to help you become conformed into the image of Jesus Christ. God doesn't do anything TO you, He allows it FOR you. Trust God no matter what!

PART III

HOW TO HANDLE TRIALS

Chapter 5

What You Think Matters

Romans 12:1-2

*I beseech you therefore, brethren, by the mercies of God, that you present your bodies a living sacrifice, holy, acceptable to God, which is your reasonable service. 2 And do not be conformed to this world, but **be transformed by the renewing of your mind**, that you may prove what is that good and acceptable and perfect will of God.* (Bold added)

What do you think when unwanted, painful events rush into your life? Do you get anxious, angry, or depressed? Do you think what is happening is unfair, unjust, or punishment from God. What do you think about?

Romans 12:1-2 teaches that we have to go through a transformation to learn to think as God thinks.

Romans 12:1 begins with "I beseech you *therefore*." Paul is here summing up what he has been saying in the previous chapters. Since there is no condemnation for those who are saved (Romans 8:1) Paul now says that Christians should *present your bodies a living sacrifice, holy, acceptable to God, which is your reasonable* [logical] *service* (Romans 12:1).

Paul continues in 12: 2, *And do not be conformed to this world, but be **transformed** by the **renewing** of your mind.* (Bold added). Let's take a closer look:

World. There are two Greek words in the New Testament that are translated *world*; *aion* which refers to an age and *cosmos* which refers to the universe. In this passage the greek word *aion* is used. So, Paul is saying do not be conformed to the *age* in which you are living.

Transformed. The Greek word for *transformed* is **metamorphoo** (from which we get **metamorphosis**). The word appears only twice in the New Testament; Romans 12:2 and II Corinthians 3:18. According to *Strong's Hebrew and Greek Dictionary* the word means *to change into a wholly different form or appearance*. The Greek word *transformed* is a command in the present tense which means to *keep on being* transformed.

Renewing. The greek word for *renewing,* according to *Thayer's Greek Definitions*, is defined as "*a renewal, renovation, complete change for the better.*" When you renovate something you take out the old and put in something better; like renovating a house. Here, we are to renovate our thinking, that is change what we are thinking.

So, let's think about trials the way God thinks. Review Chapter 2 for the nine reasons we have trials and suffering.

Now remember two important passages: I Peter 4:12, don't be surprised and Romans 8: 28, you are being conformed into the image of Christ.

This is God's thinking about trials and suffering. If you think like this you will not get anxious, angry, or depressed. If you think like this you will see God work in your situation so trust God no matter what.

Dr. Tom Constable states the following in his notes on Romans 12:1-2:

> This re-programming of the mind does not take place overnight but is a lifelong process by which our way of thinking is to resemble more and more the way God wants us to think.

The butterfly

God has given us an example of transformation in nature. Every butterfly begins life as a caterpillar; it goes through a *transformation* and becomes a completely different life form. Once the process has begun for the caterpillar there is great struggle in the cocoon. The struggle continues for hours, days, and even weeks as the caterpillar moves toward the goal of becoming a butterfly. It does not happen instantly, it takes time. This is what every believer experiences when their thinking changes; it's a struggle and it takes time.

This book is about aligning your thinking to the way God views what you should do during a trial.

How do I know if I've been transformed?

When you are willing to think like God thinks you will be changed through the work of the Holy Spirit. Transformation is, therefore, *not* something that *you do,* it is something that *happens* to *you* as you change what you think. Transformation takes place one Biblical truth at a time.

When you no longer get angry, you have been transformed by the Spirit of God. When you no longer get anxious, you have been transformed by the Spirit of God. When you no longer routinely get depressed, you have been transformed by the Spirit of God. So, as long as you do these things transformation has not been accomplished. Remember, it takes time.

Biblical Thinking

In order to grow spiritually I must *replace* the way I think with the way God thinks. Trust God no matter what!

Chapter 6

Be Doers of The Word

James 1:22

*But be doers of the word, and not hearers
only, deceiving yourselves.*

It is not enough to *know* the passages covered throughout this
book (or the rest of the Bible). It is not enough to be able to *quote*
these passages and even *explain* what each one means.

Now, don't misunderstand, it is a good thing to be able to
quote and explain a passage. But if that is all you do then you
are deceived. You must *do* what each one of these passages are
teaching.

I'll explain. In Genesis 2:16-17 we are given the account of
man's creation. God then created a garden and put the man in it to
oversee and manage. In the garden was "the tree of the knowledge
of good and evil." God commanded Adam not to eat of that tree
and if he did he would die, Genesis 2:17.

The command was not repeated. God then created the woman
to help Adam do the work in the garden. Once the woman saw
the tree she decided to eat of it's fruit while Adam was standing
beside her. He did not stop her from eating the fruit and took a bite
himself. This resulted in sin entering the human race. When God
confronted Adam he immediately blame-shifted! He blamed it on

God and the woman that He had given him, Genesis 3:13. When God confronted the woman she blamed her actions on being *deceived* by the serpent, Genesis 3:14.

The Hebrew word translated *deceived* includes in the definition the term *beguiled*. The point is this, both the man and the woman *knew what to do but they did **not** do* it. They were ***deceived*** that it was good for them!

Many agree that the book of James was the first book written in the New Testament. The first written message of the New Testament included in the first chapter a warning to ***do*** what God said, James 1:22:

> *But be doers of the word, and not*
> *hearers only, deceiving yourselves.*

"Be doers of the word" is a command just as it was in Genesis 2:17. The Greek word translated *deceived* also includes in it's definition the word *beguiled*. Now God made it clear in the opening of the Old Testament and the beginning of the New Testament that if you know what to do and you do not do it, you are *deceived, beguiled*. This means what you know is useless until you actually do it!

An automobile is a wonderful thing to have. They all come with a key to start the engine. You can have the key in you pocket or purse but until you use the key to actually start the engine the car is useless to you. If you are thirsty and hold a glass of water in your hand you will continue to be thirsty until you drink the water!

God is saying that if you know and quote the Scripture but do not do it, it is completely useless to you. You might impress other people with your knowledge but you will not impress God nor will you grow spiritually. James 4:17 noted this truth when he said:

> *Therefore, to him who knows to do good*
> *and does not do it, to him it is sin.*

In the following chapters there are passages that will get you through the storms of your life if practiced. In order for God's truth to work for you *do* what He says. I am living proof that it works. This is why I'm writing this book. I've had tremendous storms in my life as perhaps you too have experienced. Your storms may be the reason you are looking for answers. I looked to His Word to get his guidance and found answers in the passages discussed in this book.

What is outlined in this book is hard to do. It's not easy because you have to be willing to trust God for the outcome of the trial you're in. It may turn out favorable or not. You are trusting God to do what He knows is best.

He came out of the chair!

I was explaining to a young man that he needed to stop getting irritated at others, specifically his wife. I explained that love doesn't act that way. He literally came out of where he was sitting and said with great emotion, "It's not my nature to do that!" I responded with, "You're right, it's not your nature, that's why you need to let

God work in your heart."

Biblical Thinking

Knowing what God has written in the Bible is not enough, you must *do* what God has said. Trust God no matter what!

Chapter 7

How Do I Count It All Joy?

James 1:2-4

My brethren, count it all joy when you fall into various trials, 3 knowing that the testing of your faith produces patience. 4 But let patience have its perfect work, that you may be perfect and complete, lacking nothing.

According to scholars the book of James was written somewhere between 45 and 50 A.D. That makes James the first book written in the New Testament collection. Since this was the first book written it carries with it great significance because the first written message delivered to Christians from God was how to understand and handle trials.

James starts by telling Christians that it is a joyous occasion to be experiencing trials! Wait! What? Why would he say that? That's encouragement? Is James saying that we should be happy and throw a block party and do cart wheels in the streets when we are experiencing difficulties? Is James saying to not express sadness and to act as if nothing is happening?

It is difficult for you to see *joy* when you're hurting. Does God really expect you to do that? Your reaction to "count it all joy" may have been the same as mine when I first read this verse as a young Christian.

31

Frankly, the idea did not make sense to me. I thought I did not understand it because I was a young believer.

One day I decided to check out the definition of the Greek word *chara* which is here translated *joy*. The Greek word *chara* actually means *calm delight*. When I understood that the passage then made perfect sense!

It does *not* mean to be happy and throw a party with balloons. It doesn't mean that I shouldn't feel emotions of sadness because of what has happened. It means that I should have *calmness* about what is happening. Why? Read on and you will discover that the trial you're in is designed to produce *endurance* and endurance produces *maturity*.

When you're going through a trial why should you have *calm delight*? Because **God is at work in your life** as the rest of the passage says. It continues, "*Knowing that the testing of your faith produces patience.*" The goal of testing is not to destroy but to *refine*. The only other time this greek word appears in the New Testament is in I Peter 1:7. *Testing* there is illustrated by gold being purified by fire. The impurities are separated from the gold making the gold more valuable. The benefit of testing then is to rid the believer of impurities.

If you endure the trial there is more benefit. Testing produces *patience*. According to *Thayer Greek Definitions* the word *refers to the characteristic of a man who is not swerved from his deliberate purpose and his loyalty to faith and piety by even the greatest trials and sufferings, a patient enduring, sustaining, perseverance.* The benefit of a trial has the potential of producing in you patient endurance while waiting on God to do His work in you. God produces maturity in those believers who do not run from a trial but who endures the circumstances.

Bible teacher and author Warren Wiersbe tells the story of being taught what farmers do while he was in grade school. He, like the other students, had been raised in the city and they were clueless as to what farmers did to grow crops. So the wise teacher gave each student a small flower pot, some dirt, and a seed to plant. She instructed that they were responsible to fill the flower pot with the dirt, plant the seed, give it water and sun every day. Warren said he was so curious as to how the seed was doing that he would dig it up everyday! To no ones surprise, except Warren, the seed never grew. Warren said what he learned from that experience to "bloom where you are planted." If you stay where you are (endure) you will grow toward maturity.

My first experience with calm delight

I became a Christian when I was a teenager. Within a short period of time I believed God was calling me into the ministry. That was unsettling for me because my brother had told me that a call to ministry was a call to prepare! That was my problem! To say that I didn't like school was an understatement. I barely made it out of high school. The thought that I had to go to college and beyond had zero appeal to me. Zero!

I struggled with the Lord and told Him that I would go into the ministry but I didn't want to go to college. I thought He agreed. I had peace. My mistake!

After I graduated from high school I ran from the Lord and joined the Air Force. I was raised in Pensacola Florida and where did the Lord send me? Grand Forks, North Dakota. I should have known then that God was trying to get my attention but I didn't. The coldest temperature I had experienced in Florida was 27 degrees. The coldest I experienced in North Dakota was -38 degrees below zero (not wind chill)!

I was already married when I joined the Air Force and had a baby a few months old when God finally got my attention. This was around 1963 and the pay for an enlisted man wasn't much but I was were able to squeeze out $5.00 to buy a used TV (no, the amount is correct). We lived in the third floor attic apartment.

One evening we were watching TV with the volume down low trying not to wake our baby girl, Kathy, when I heard a noise. I asked my wife "Did you hear that?" She said she did not. A few minutes passed and I heard a popping sound twice. I asked her if she had heard that. She said maybe. Quickly I heard three popping sounds close to each other, "Pop, Pop, Pop!" I quickly ran to be back of the apartment and opened the closet door. There was a small built-in cabinet on the floor and when I opened the doors I was met with an explosion of flames and smoke! The house was on fire and spreading quickly! We called the fire department and escaped the house with our baby and the clothes on our back. The popping sounds I heard were light bulbs bursting from the heat!

It was twelve degrees outside with snow on the ground. I was standing on the sidewalk without a jacket watching everything we had go up in flames. The wife and baby were covered and protected. I remember looking at the smoke bellowing out of our window and I had a peace about me that I could not explain.

I knew exactly why the house was on fire, I was running from the Lord. He wanted me to go to college and I joined the military!

So standing on the sidewalk I said to the Lord, "Okay, I'll go to school." I was not upset, I had "calm delight" because I knew God was getting my attention. By the way, our apartment was the only one severely damaged by fire. The apartment below us had only slight water damage.

Fifty-three years later I decided to return to the city of Grand Forks, North Dakota. I wanted to see if the house was still there. It took only about ten minutes in the city to find the house! The only thing that was different was the color. I took pictures as I relived the moment the house was burning. I pulled across the street and was about to leave when I stopped, turned the car off, and walked across the street.

I was now standing on the exact same spot on the sidewalk where I stood over half a century before. I bowed my head, wept and said, "Lord I did it, I went to school." Now, you and I both know The Lord knew that I went to school! It was just my way of saying to Him "Thank You" for getting my attention and giving me calmness in the middle of the trial. I wanted to pile up some rocks like the did in the Old Testament to mark a sacred spot!

Because God gave me *calm delight* while the apartment was on fire it helped me want the same peace when going through other trials that followed.

Colossians 1:9-14

Paul wrote Colossians while he was in prison around 60 A.D. He had not been to the city but he was writing to encourage them in the faith and to speak about the false teaching to which they had been exposed.

In his introduction Paul prayed a magnificent prayer in which he asked that they would be strengthened with power so they would be *patient* through *longsuffering* with *joy* (Colossians 1:11). Paul prayed for them to *endure* through the tough times they were experiencing but do it with *joy*. It's the same word for *joy* that James and Peter uses and means *calm delight*. Paul is saying have *calm delight* because God is giving you the power to endure!

Biblical Thinking

God is at work in your life in any trial big or small. Ask God to give you **calm delight** in your trial and thank Him for working in your current circumstances. Trust God no matter what!

Chapter 8

Do Not Get Angry

Ephesians 4:26

*Be angry, and do not sin": do not let
the sun go down on your wrath...*

In the next three chapters we will be discussing anger, anxiety, and depression. Each one of these, when allowed, will *distract* you from allowing God to work to accomplish His will in your trial.

When a disturbing event happens without warning the first response is usually *shock*. "What! I can't believe that this is happening," "I do not understand what God is doing to me!" or "Why do these things always happen to me?"

When the shock wares off, anger often takes it's place. The anger is usually directed toward God or the person/persons that caused the situation. Anger brings with it the view that your circumstances are not fair or this is punishment from God. When you are angry you will be *distracted* from seeing God's goodness and grace in your circumstance.

Not all anger is sin
If you are the recipient of an injustice that is causing the problem it's appropriate to be angry. But it's not appropriate to hang onto the anger. Deal with it quickly. According to Ephesians 4:26

getting angry is commanded. Jesus said that if you're angry be sure you have a cause (Matthew 5:22), i.e., not selfish anger.

Righteous indignation is appropriate anger when directed toward an injustice as Jesus did when He threw out the money changers from the temple, Matthew 21:12-13:

> *Then Jesus went into the temple of God and drove out all those who bought and sold in the temple, and overturned the tables of the money changers and the seats of those who sold doves. 13 And He said to them, "It is written, 'My house shall be called a house of prayer,' but you have made it a 'den of thieves.'"*

Even when anger is justified we are still instructed to deal with it quickly or as Paul said in Ephesians 4:26, *do not let the sun go down on your wrath nor give place to the devil.*

By not letting our anger go we are giving a place for Satan to work. How would Satan work? Anger will keep your focus on the injustice and the individual or individuals that caused what is happening instead of on God! Anger takes God out of your focus and puts it on the problem you're facing. Here is what Solomon said in Ecclesiastes 7:9...

> *Do not hasten in your spirit to be angry,*
> *For anger rests in the bosom of fools.*

The word fool here means, "stupid, silly, foolish." This is saying that being angry is senseless, silly, of no value. Here is the CEV translation of this verse:

Only fools get angry quickly
and hold a grudge.

The Bible is clear, even when justified, do not hang on to your anger, let it go quickly. My brother, Mike, wrote the following in his published booklet, *Anger*:

> The Bible has several things to say about dealing with anger. In the context of dealing with trials, James says, be "slow to wrath" (James 1:19). Concerning dealing with anger as well as other sins, Paul says, "Put them away" (Ephesians 4:31). Even after giving the command to be angry and not sin, Paul says, "Do not let the sun go down on your wrath" (Ephesians 4:26). In other words, the Scripture instructs angry people, even when it is righteous indignation, to deal with the anger. Angry people are responsible for seeing to it that they properly deal with their anger. In the case of righteous indignation, angry people are not responsible for what causes the anger, but even in those cases, they are responsible for not letting anger linger or develop into such things as resentment.

James 1:19-21

Anger is not an option. James, the half-brother of Christ, wrote a letter to encourage the Jews that had been dispersed. They were having trials and James wanted them to understand *why,* what *to do*, and what *not to do*.

In chapter one James is explaining the purpose of trials and gives guidance as how to respond and how not to respond. James is saying that the reason for trials is to produce maturity (Christ likeness). So be patient and let the trial do its work. James in

1:19-20 warns them *not to be angry* over what is happening:

> *So then, my beloved brethren, let every man be swift to hear, slow to speak, slow to wrath; for the wrath of man does not produce the righteousness of God.*

If you get angry about the difficulties you experience you will miss the righteousness of God that is being taught in the trial. You are to receive the Word with *meekness* (James 1:21):

> *Therefore lay aside all filthiness and overflow of wickedness, and receive with meekness the implanted word, which is able to save your souls.*

More verses on anger:

Proverbs 14:29 *A patient man has great understanding, but a quick-tempered man displays folly.*

Proverbs 15:1 *A gentle answer turns away wrath, but a harsh word stirs up anger.*

Proverbs 15:18 *A hot-tempered person stirs up conflict, but the one who is patient calms a quarrel.*

Proverbs 16:32 *Better a patient man than a warrior, a man who controls his temper than one who takes a city.*

Proverbs 29:11 *A fool gives full vent to his anger, but a wise man keeps himself under control.*

I Corinthians 13: 5 *Love is not provoked* (means that love does not get irritated).

Colossians 3:8 *But now you must rid yourselves of all such things as these: anger, rage, malice, slander, and filthy language from your lips."*

Biblical Thinking
Do not hold on to anger, quickly let it go. Trust God no matter what!

Chapter 9

Do Not Be Anxious

Philippians 4:5-6

Be anxious for nothing, but in everything by prayer and supplication, with thanksgiving, let your requests be made known to God; 7 and the peace of God, which supasses all understanding, will guard your hearts and minds through Christ Jesus.

Anxiety, like anger, when allowed to continue, will *distract* you from seeing God work in your circumstances.

Of course, opportunities to become anxious are easy to find when you are experiencing life's trials. Any level of anxiety can paralyze you into not thinking clearly or Biblically. The question is what can be done when you are feeling anxious about what is happening in your life? The issue of not getting anxious is mentioned several times in the Bible but the most popular passage is Philippians 4:6-7.

Let's unpack these verses and discover the truth that God wants you to practice. The Greek word in Philippians 4:6 translated "anxious" means *care*. According to *Vine's Expository Dictionary of New Testament Words*, *care* means "to draw in different directions, *distract*, hence signifies that which causes this, a care, especially an anxious care." The word *care* then holds the idea to be drawn away by caring too much which causes a *distraction*. Paul is not

43

saying to *not* care, he is saying do not care to the point that you are *distracted.* But distracted from what? You are distracted from **involving God** in what is concerning you.

Notice that the phrase *be anxious for nothing* in verse 4 is immediately followed by Paul telling us to *pray.* So when you pray you are **involving God** in what is going on that is causing you anxious care. Notice also that your prayer is to include *thanksgiving.* That means that you pray thanking God for the outcome...whatever it is, weather it's to your liking or not! Leave the outcome to God because He knows what is best for you.

The word for "*nothing*" means "not one whit." So nothing literally means nothing. When you take *everything* away from something you are left with *nothing.* Paul is saying there is *nothing* for which you are to be *anxious* or *distracted.* Now, the tense of this Greek word "nothing" is prohibiting an action that is already underway. So Paul is saying to the Christians in Philippi *you are distracted because you are carrying too much so stop it!*

Notice the contrast between being anxious for *nothing* and praying for *everything.* Two completely opposite extremes. Nothing means nothing and everything means everything. There is nothing over which you are to be anxious and you are not to overlook anything for which you are to pray. Read that again!

As you read on in the verse you find that when you pray *with thanksgiving* God will give you peace to guard both your *emotions* (heart) and *mind*! Guard you from what? You will be guarded from being *anxious*! And Paul adds that the peace is so terrific that it will *exceed* anything you could understand or imagine!

Actually, you can't explain what's it's like, it has to be experienced.

If you want God's peace *involve* Him in what you are going through by praying *with thanksgiving*. Be willing to accept whatever He does. This is what it means to pray with thanksgiving.

The truth of Philippians 4:6-7 has wide implications and application. When you fail to *involve God* in what is causing you *anxious concern* you will be *distracted* from what God is doing in your life. When you are anxious, you are not accepting the trial as being used of God to conform you into the image of His Son.

Instead, you will be surprised and overwhelmed at what is happening and you forfeit the opportunity to experience God's grace, mercy, and peace. All of this happens when you fail to *involve God* in your trial and get anxious and therefore distracted.

When you are distracted by anxiety you question the goodness of God and conclude that life isn't fair or it just doesn't make sense. You can prevent all of that from happening when you *involve God* in your concerns by prayer. God will then grant you peace and will guard your heart and mind from crippling anxiety.

To *not* be anxious is a command not a suggestion. Paul is saying STOP being anxious. Since it is a command it is possible for you to choose to not be anxious. So, if you want to get beyond being anxious about anything and everything, then make the *choice* to quote this verse the very moment you find yourself getting anxious and then make a *choice* to not be *distracted* by being worried.

Give the situation to God and let Him do as He wills. God will grant you peace because He honors His Word and He will meet you at the point of obedience with peace.

If you choose to not be anxious with the small things that happen you will be able to do the same when the big events rush into your life. Philippians 4:6-7 is so key to growing spiritually that its importance cannot be overstated. The anxiety battle must be won to prevent missing what God has for you. Be prepared and practice Philippians 4:6-7 daily.

Matthew 6:31-34

In this passage Jesus tells us not to be *anxious* about anything. Paul used the same Greek word for *anxious* (merimnao) as Jesus did which holds the idea of being drawn away by caring too much which causes a distraction.

Jesus is saying you are distracted from seeking His kingdom and His righteousness when you worry about what you are going to eat, drink, wear, or even tomorrow. The Scripture is clear, Christian's are never to be anxious about anything at anytime.

> *Therefore do not worry, saying, 'What shall we eat?' or 'What shall we drink?' or 'What shall we wear?' For after all these things the Gentiles seek. For your heavenly Father knows that you need all these things. But seek first the kingdom of God and His righteousness, and all these things shall be added to you. Therefore do not worry about tomorrow, for tomorrow will worry about its own things. Sufficient for the day is its own trouble.*

Biblical Thinking

I am not to be anxious about *anything* because God is in control of *everything*, even my current situation. Trust God no matter what!

Chapter 10

Do Not Fear

Psalm 23

The Lord is my shepherd; I shall not want. 2 He makes me to lie down in green pastures; He leads me beside the still waters. 3 He restores my soul; He leads me in the paths of righteousness For His name's sake. 4 Yea, though I walk through the valley of the shadow of death, I will fear no evil; For You are with me; Your rod and Your staff, they comfort me. 5 You prepare a table before me in the presence of my enemies; You anoint my head with oil; My cup runs over. 6 Surely goodness and mercy shall follow me All the days of my life; And I will dwell in the house of the Lord Forever.

Psalm 23 is the most quoted passage in all of the Bible. We are uncentain of the backdrop of why this psalm was written or when. It appears, however, that David wrote this brief psalm not in the beginning of his life but toward the end. It seems as though he is reflecting over his life to be reminded of how God had been with him every step of the way.

He begins in verse 1 with the conclusion of his reflection, *The Lord is my shepherd; I shall not want.* After thinking about it David decided God, as his Shepherd, was all that he ever needed.

Now, through the eyes of a sheep, he records how the Shepherd has provided for him throughout his life. God has provided for his:

Physical needs:

> Verse 2 *He makes me to lie down in green pastures; He leads me beside the still waters.*

Green grass to a sheep is like eating a filet mignon steak, it is the best. Still waters represent the compassion of the shepherd. Mountain streams created noise because of the rushing water going down hill over rocks. A caring shepherd blocked off an area where the water would gather and be calm so as to not frighten the sheep.

Spiritual needs:

> Verse 3 *He restores my soul; He leads me in the paths of righteousness For His name's sake.*

When a sheep would wander away from the flock a caring shepherd would get the sheep and restore in to the safety of the flock.

Emotional needs:

> Verse 4 *Yea, though I walk through the valley of the shadow of death, I will fear no evil; For You are with me; Your rod and Your staff, they comfort me. 5 You prepare a table before me in the presence of my enemies; You anoint my head with oil; My cup runs over.*

Notice that there is a suddenly change the language. He has been talking *about* the Shepherd but now he starts talking *to* the Shepherd.

David remembers the many times he faced death and he refers to it as a mere shadow; *shadow of death.* Someone has said it is better to be hit by the shadow of a moving truck than the truck!

David remembers that God had tools to help him in his trouble, the rod and staff. David is overwhelmed at God's provisions that he says his cup runs over. God has provided abudantly!

Future needs:

Verse 6 *Surely goodness and mercy shall follow me All the days of my life; And I will dwell in the house of the Lord Forever.*

David is overwhelmed since God *has* provided for him He *will* provide for him in the future.

David learned to trust God even in the face of death and he learned not to fear evil!

Going through a trial makes it easy to become fearful about what *may* happen. David learned to not fear evil after facing it many times over his life. David saw God deliever him time after time so his confidence grew over the years to not fear regardless of his situation.

This trial you're in right now may be an opportunity to see God deliever you from evil. Trust God to protect and redeem you from whatever situation you are facing.

This Psalm has helped millions of Christians since it was written over 3,000 years ago and it can help you. Say with David, *I will not fear evil because You are with me.*

Biblical Thinking

I will not fear evil because God is with me. Trust God no matter what!

Chapter 11

Do Not Get Depressed

Proverbs 12:25

*Anxiety in the heart of man causes depression,
But a good word makes it glad.*

When you allow anger and anxiety into your life it will invariably lead to being depressed and feeling overwhelmed.

Depression is a feeling of sadness and dejection that altars a person's emotional and mental state and interferes with their daily life functions in varying degrees. Being depressed signals giving up hope for a good outcome of your situation. Symptoms range from mild to severe and can be short term or last for an extended period of time.

Before I go further please understand that some *sad feelings* are appropriate, normal, and expected. For example, if you were to loose a loved one to death it would be expected to feel deeply sad emotions and have normal activities like eating, sleeping and working interrupted. After a period of time these functions return to normal and you will continue your journey through this life.

For the most part, however, those who report they are "depressed" are focused on one or more problems. Life has over-whelmed them, a tragic event has happened, or something did not happened as expected, someone did something to them, or they did something to someone else...the list is endless.

It is different when a Christian *routinely* gets depressed over the painful events in their life. It is different when the Christian *routinely* retreats and withdraws from life to pout or fume about their circumstances. It is different when a Christian *routinely* reacts negatively to events, gets angry, anxious, and depressed.

When depression is a normal response to difficulties of life people are living examples of what the stoic philosopher Epictetus (A.D. c. 55–135) said nearly 2,000 years ago,

People are disturbed, not by things or events, but by the views (perceptions) which they take of them.

What disturbs you is not *what* happens but what you *think* about what happens. It's not the event, it's what you *think* about the event...it's your perception.

People who get depressed disturb themselves by rehearsing their negative thoughts (perceptions) of the event. Depressed people therefore...

...think too much about the wrong thing.

People who are depressed are *not* trying to *solve* the problem, they are embedded *in* the problem by reviewing the *negatives* and fuming over the *wrongness* of the event. People who are depressed are therefore *choosing* to be miserable.

If you routinely react this way to life's problems it is because you fail to see that God is working through your circumstances to conform you into the image of His Son (Romans 8:28-29). Instead of seeing God in the situation, you are viewing your circumstance as not fair, wrong, or even punishment from God.

The unfairness or wrongness is what is being reviewed and rehearsed in your thinking. All you can see is the pain and suffering you are going through and you want it to stop...now! Christians that get depressed are stuck in, and focused on, the problem. Christians who get depressed fail to see or do not accept what God is doing in their life through their circumstances.

Jonah 1:1-4:11

Jonah is an example of what happens when you don't accept what God is doing in your life. The Lord told Jonah to go the Nineveh and preach repentance. Jonah did not think that was such a good idea because the Ninivites were enemies of Israel and he wanted to see them destroyed not spared. So he bought a ticket on a boat going somewhere, it did not matter where. The Lord then sent a storm (Jonah 1:4) to get Jonah's attention. (May I pause to say that this is exactly the purpose of any storm that moves into your life... God is trying to get your attention.)

Well the crew eventually figured out that the problem was Jonah (Jonah 1:7) and he was thrown overboard (Jonah 1:15). We know what happened next; a rather large fish swallowed Jonah. This was another attention getting maneuver and the second attempt worked.

Jonah prayed (Jonah 2:1)! God answered his prayer and the fish spit Jonah out onto dry land. With his new enlightenment Jonah headed to Nineveh and delivered the message God had given him (Jonah 3:4).

Jonah's message from God was received and the city repented (Jonah 3:5-10). But again, Jonah reacted with rebellion and anger toward God at what He was doing (Jonah 4:1) and then he became depressed (Jonah 4:8-9). When God did not do what Jonah wanted Him to do he wanted to die.

Blinded by these emotions Jonah could not see that God was doing something not only for Nineveh but for him. God demonstrated His Grace to Nineveh and Jonah missed the lesson.

These emotions expressed by Jonah are not uncommon among Christians that are displeased or confused about what God is doing in their life. We are not to be dismayed according to Deuteronomy 31:8...

It is the LORD who goes before you. He will be with you; he will not leave you or forsake you. Do not fear or be dismayed.

The Hebrew word translated *leave* has the idea of *leave alone*. The word that immediately follows is *forsake* which means to *leave destitute or fail*. The Hebrew word for *dismayed* means to break down either by confusion and fear, hence to be discouraged or, literally, to be terrified.

Moses, who wrote Deuteronomy, has given us three reasons to not be discouraged or depressed. First, God goes *before* you which means He holds the future and He is leading you. Second, He is *with* you which means He is *beside* you. Thirdly, He will never *fail* you or *leave* you *destitute*. With a promise like this there is no reason to ever be discouraged or depressed. God is there for you and always will be. Trust Him no matter what!

There are no happy depressed people

In my years as a therapist I never met a happy depressed person. People that came to me with the symptoms of depression are dealing with a disappointing life event and they are *stuck*.

I have also never dealt with anyone that reported symptoms of depression who was *unable to identify* an event that was causing their emotional pain.

Christians open the door to depression when they fail to obey Philippians 4:6-7, become anxious about their concern, and do not involved God by giving the situation to Him. Depressed Christians do not take *God's view* about their concerns.

As soon as you accept that God is at work and you see the circumstance from His point of view you will no longer be depressed. When you fail to recognize and *involve* the Lord in your life you forfeit peace, growth, and His blessings.

A remarkable reversal

I worked at a mental hospital in Dallas, Texas. I was routinely called to evaluate people that were in one of nine hospital emergency rooms in Dallas County. At 2 A.M. I was called to evaluate a young man to see if he needed to be committed to our facility for treatment. Upon arrival, the ER doctor briefed me on what had happened.

The young man's wife had left him and she was living in a crack house addicted to cocaine. He had tried everything to get her back but he had failed. He stopped eating and was severely depressed. He was actually starving himself to death over his grief and love for his wife. Out of desperation his sister brought him to the hospital emergency room. Here's what happened.

His sister told me that her brother and his wife were both Christians. He was sitting in the back of the room with a blanket over his head. At first he would not talk to me or even look at me, he just sat there with his head covered.

I asked his sister if I could talk to him about the Bible (she was holding one under her arm). She said yes. I explained to him that God cared more about her than he did and that this was God's problem to solve, not his. He had exhausted all of his efforts and now it was time to let God take over. I encouraged him to let God take care of his wayward wife and for him to trust God in what seemed to be an impossible situation. He did not respond.

I turned my attention back to his sister again and after a few minutes had passed I looked over and he had stood up. His continence was hopeful. He said, "This is not my problem, it is God's problem!" Turning his attention now to his sister he said, "I'm hungry, can we get something to eat!" This young man made a remarkable reversal of his emotional state when he made the decision to let God solve his problem.

Summary

When trials come into your life and you do not accept the circumstances as coming from God you open the door to becoming anxious and angry about what is happening. When you allow anxiety to control you it leads to depression. When you become *anxious, angry, and depressed* over life's troubles you *remove* God showing you mercy and grace. You will be distracted from seeing God's purpose for the event.

When you do not accept that God is conforming you into the image of His Son you will be surprised and distracted from what God is doing in your life. You will not be patient, nor will you trust the Lord, you will then forfeit peace and will not grow spiritually. By accepting that God is at work in your life through your circumstances you allow God to do His work in creating His likeness in you.

Biblical Thinking

God is working in my life to conform me into the image of His Son. There is no reason why I should be depressed. So, I will trust God no matter what!

If you are angry
you're living in past.

If you are anxious
you're living in the future.

If you are depressed you're
thinking about the wrong thing.

If you have peace
you're living in the present
and trusting God.

Chapter 12

Forgive

Ephesians 4:31-32

Let all bitterness and wrath and anger and clamor and slander be put away from you, along with all malice. Be kind to one another, tenderhearted, forgiving one another, as God in Christ forgave you.

Being in a trial is never easy (understatement). There is so much to learn from the way God is working. But we usually don't see God's grace working at first.

One of the most challenging requirements as a christian to do is forgive the one who has wronged you. I write this out of my own experience because I also understand the greater the offence the greater the difficulty to forgive.

What did God say about forgiving others? First, lets look at what Jesus did while he was being crucified. He was hanging on the cross and said this as recorded in Luke 23:34...

Father, forgive them, for they
do not know what they do.

Jesus is our example to follow. Even while hanging on the cross He asked the Father to forgive those responsible. The word *forgive* here here means "to let go, disregard." Jesus was asking

God the Father to disregard what they were doing to Him while it was happenng!

In Ephesians 4:31-32 a different Greek word is used for *forgive*; here it means *to grant forgiveness, to pardon.* It both cases the idea is *to let it go, don't hold something against another person.*

So, if what you are going through is because of someone causing you problems we are instructed to forgive that person or persons. Let it go. Here is what I say when someone has wronged me...

> No one can do anything to me that is grater than
> what I did to Jesus. I sent Him to the cross!

You do not have the right to withold forgiving anyone for anything because God has forgiven you for everything. So, find it in your heart to forgive the person or persons that has wronged you and ask God for the grace to do so.

Erica Kirk

Charles James Kirk (October 14, 1993 – September 10, 2025) was an American right-wing political activist and media personality. He co-founded the conservative student organization Turning Point USA (TPUSA) in 2012 and served as its executive director until his assassination in 2025.

Erica Kirk (wife), spoke at Charlie Kirk's memorial and announced that she had forgiven the one who killed him.

Biblical Thinking

Difficult as it can be, you are to forgive others because God has forgiven you. May God grant you the grace to forgive those who have wronged you. Trust God no matter what!

Chapter 13

Come Boldly To The Throne of Grace

Hebrews 4:14-16

Seeing then that we have a great High Priest who has passed through the heavens, Jesus the Son of God, let us hold fast our confession. 15 For we do not have a High Priest who cannot sympathize with our weaknesses, but was in all points tempted as we are, yet without sin. 16 Let us therefore come boldly to the throne of grace, that we may obtain mercy and find grace to help in time of need.

Are you are hurting, feeling overwhelmed, feeling misunderstood, feeling guilty? You are invited to come *boldly* to the throne of grace to to ask for *mercy* and *grace*!

You do not have to be innocent of wrong doing to come boldly to God's throne. The reason to go to God's throne is to get mercy and grace regardless of why!

Asking for *mercy* is asking God to *not give you what you deserve*! Asking for grace is asking God to *give you what you don't deserve*! Read the last two sentences again! God is willing to withhold what you deserve and give you what you don't deserve!

God has given us permission to approach Him *boldly*. The word *bold* means to be *frank, blunt, and confident*. How is this possible? First, Jesus is our High Priest which means He is in the position to help. Second, He understands our weaknesses, He actually *sympathizes with our weaknesses*. Why? Because He too was tempted, *For we do not have a High Priest who cannot sympathize with our weaknesses, but was in all points tempted as we are, yet without sin.*

We are weak and make bad choices. Jesus understands that and because of that He offers help even when we have acted sinfully.

I was facing an IRS audit over thirty years ago. They asked me something for which I did not have the answer. I was perplexed on knowing what to do. So, I cried out to the Lord in utter despair and desperation! I literally screamed out loud "Lord I need an answer, If You can't help me then who can? In less than a second the answer popped into my head! I thought, "Wow, thank you Lord! I had boldly approached the Throne of Grace and He answered me. He was just waiting for me to ask!

That's what He wants you to do! Ask Him! God has given you permission to approach Him. He has open the door and said to you "Come on in and ask Me for mercy and grace!" Ask Him for anything but ask Him clearly, plainly, and boldly.

Biblical Thinking

Regardless of your need, you are invited to ask God for His mercy and grace in your situation. Trust God no matter what!

Chapter 14

Ask For Wisdom

James 1:5-8

5 If any of you lacks wisdom, let him ask of God, who gives to all liberally and without reproach, and it will be given to him. 6 But let him ask in faith, with no doubting, for he who doubts is like a wave of the sea driven and tossed by the wind. 7 For let not that man suppose that he will receive anything from the Lord; 8 he is a double-minded man, unstable in all his ways.

Going through a trial is often confusing and overwhelming. "Why is this happening, why now, why me, why this, and what am I suppose to learn? I just don't get it! I need help!"

Remember that James is the first book written in the New Testament and he starts off talking about the purpose of trials and how to best understand the challenge.

Remember too that he said count it all joy which means to recognize that God is at work in your life so be at peace, have calm delight.

If you do not understand why this is happening in your life James encourages you to ask God for wisdom. He will show you why this is happening and He will not treat you poorly. Be patient and wait on the Lord to give you an answer. He will in His time.

Young girl ask for wisdom

I was counseling a ten year old girl with her family because she had just found out that she had been adopted. She was deeply bothered.

I explained to her that she was a lucky young girl. She was a Christian and I explained that she had been adopted into God's family and then adopted by her father who was sitting there. I said, "You've been adopted twice! Wow, you are really loved by God and your dad!" She cried!

She was very intelligent and had good questions. I suggested that she ask God to give her wisdom. She thought about it but asked what was up there over the balcony? I said why don't you go see. She walked up the stairs to investigate. I think she wanted some time alone to ponder the question. Her mother and I kept talking for about ten minutes. She came to edge of the balcony and said "Guess what?" I said "What?" She responded with "I just asked God for wisdom." I gave her praise for making such a decision!

I will not live long enough to see what God does in her life. I do know that God will grant her request in ways she could never imagine. At age ten she showed a heart for the Lord.

Biblical Thinking

Ask God to show you the wisdom that is necessary to deal with your trial correctly. The little girl did. Trust God no matter what!

Chapter 15

Keep On Asking!

Luke 18:1-8

Then He spoke a parable to them, that men always ought to pray and not lose heart, 2 saying: "There was in a certain city a judge who did not fear God nor regard man. 3 Now there was a widow in that city; and she came to him, saying, 'Get justice for me from my adversary.' 4 And he would not for a while; but afterward he said within himself, 'Though I do not fear God nor regard man, 5 yet because this widow troubles me I will avenge her, lest by her continual coming she weary me.' " 6 Then the Lord said, "Hear what the unjust judge said. 7 And shall God not avenge His own elect who cry out day and night to Him, though He bears long with them? 8 I tell you that He will avenge them speedily. Nevertheless, when the Son of Man comes, will He really find faith on the earth?

In James 1:5-8 we were told to ask for wisdom to deal with trials correctly. Before James penned these words Jesus used a parable to teach a moral lesson. In this story we are told to keep on asking, to not give up. What was she asking for? She was asking for justice.

The benefit in continually asking God for help is it keeps your thoughts directed toward the One who is capable of solving the problem. The more you stay focused on Him the less you will be focused on the problem. Remember what happened when Peter was walking on water toward Jesus (Matthew 14:22-33)?

And Peter answered Him and said, "Lord, if it is You, command me to come to You on the water." 29 So He said, "Come." And when Peter had come down out of the boat, he walked on the water to go to Jesus. 30 But when he saw that the wind was boisterous, he was afraid; and beginning to sink he cried out, saying, "Lord, save me!" 31 And immediately Jesus stretched out His hand and caught him, and said to him, "O you of little faith, why did you doubt?" 32 And when they got into the boat, the wind ceased.

As long as Peter was looking at Jesus he was on top of the water. But as soon as he took his eyes off Jesus he began to sink.

Notice Peter's lack of faith did not stop Jesus from showing mercy and grace to him. He stretched out His hand to keep him from drowning.

Whatever the concern that is on your heart keep asking God for help. Do as the lady in the parable did, she bugged the man in authority to help her and he did. Don't stop asking God for help.

Biblical Thinking
God wants you to keep asking Him for help. Trust God no matter what!

PART IV

BUT WHAT IF...?

Chapter 16

What If I'm Guilty

Psalm 6

A Prayer of Faith in Time of Distress

What if you caused the problems you're having? What if you are guilty of something? Is God's grace and mercy available to you? The answer is yes, of course!

Before you became a Christian you were guilty of sin that was worthy of eternal separation from God. You were under God's wrath and condemnation. But God saved you when you trusted Jesus Christ as your Savior! All sin was forgiven. According to Romans 8:1a...

> *There is therefore now no condemnation*
> *to those who are in Christ Jesus...*

So, you were guilty and God showed you mercy and grace. That same mercy and grace is still available to you even when you fail in this life!

King David in Psalm 6 was guilty of something so horrendous that out of desperation he called out to God for *mercy*. Notice what David asked for and why in Psalm 6:1-3:

71

O Lord, do not rebuke me in Your anger, Nor chasten me in Your hot displeasure. 2 Have mercy on me, O Lord, for I am weak; O Lord, heal me, for my bones are troubled. 3 My soul also is greatly troubled; But You, O Lord—how long?

David asked God to *not rebuke him* in His anger; the word rebuke means to *correct or chasten*. David continues to asked God not to *chasten* him, again, in *His hot displeasure*, which is stronger than *anger* mention before. This word means *furious*.

So David asked God not to **correct** him of out of His fierce anger. Instead David asked for **mercy**, which means *to show favor, to bend or stoop in kindness to an inferior*.

What was David's reason for asking God to not **correct** him out of His anger? David appealed to his own humanity, *Have mercy on me, O Lord, for I am* **weak**. The Hebrew word *weak* appears only here and means *sick, weak*.

Jesus recognized that the *flesh* is weak in Matthew 26:41, *Watch and pray so that you will not fall into temptation. The spirit is willing, but the flesh is weak.*

What was David's sin? We do not know for sure. My brother, Mike, wrote this in his unpublished notes about David's sin:

David pleads, "O LORD do not rebuke me in Your anger nor chasten me in Your hot displeasure" (6:1). No one knows for sure the exact circumstances behind this Psalm. From the Psalm itself, it seems that David had sinned. Perhaps, the sin was his adultery with Bathsheba. That is a guess, but it is probably a good guess. While the specifics are not known, what is clear is that David sinned, God was angry, and God chastened him.

Since the sin issue is not mentioned, it had probably been dealt with and was no longer a problem (Ps. 51). What was a problem was the chastening of God (if the sin was the adultery, the chastening was foretold by Nathan; 2 Sam. 12:10-12, 14), that is, David's sin had consequences, which affected others. His sin has been forgiven by God, but the consequence was reaping havoc in his life.

David steps up his bold approach to God and gives two reasons in verses 4 and 5 why God should pull back his discipline and deliver him. First, David reminded God that He is *merciful*. Second, God would not receive public praise if he were dead.

Return, O Lord, deliver me! Oh, save me for Your mercies' sake! 5 For in death there is no remembrance of You; In the grave who will give You thanks?

David now lets God know just how much he has already suffered physically; verses 6 and 7:

I am weary with my groaning; All night I make my bed swim; I drench my couch with my tears. 7 My eye wastes away because of grief; It grows old because of all my enemies.

God answered David's request and stopped the chastisement. Now he gives a warning to those who would harm him because of his sin.

Depart from me, all you workers of iniquity; For the Lord has heard the voice of my weeping. 9 The Lord has heard my supplication; The Lord will receive my prayer. 10 Let all my enemies be ashamed and greatly troubled; Let them turn back and be ashamed suddenly.

Why is this Psalm significant?

The Psalm is extremely significant for those who have caused their own problem. There will always be consequences for your behavior. We are warned in the Old Testament that we get what we deserve; Proverbs 11:18...

> *The wicked man does deceptive work, But he who sows righteousness will have a sure reward.*

This is equivalent to what the Apostle Paul said thousands of years later in Galatians 6:7-8...

Do not be deceived, God is not mocked; for whatever a man sows, that he will also reap. 8 For he who sows to his flesh will of the flesh reap corruption, but he who sows to the Spirit will of the Spirit reap everlasting life.

But wait, David was a man after God's own heart and he greatly sinned? Samuel was speaking about David when he said in I Samuel 13:14...

But now your kingdom shall not continue. The Lord has sought for Himself a man after His own heart, and the Lord has commanded him to be commander over His people...

Psalm 6 was probably written after David's affair with Bathsheba and the murder of her husband, Uriah. Now, since David was a man after God's own heart (mentioned also in Acts 13:22) so how could he commit the sin with Bathsheba and the sin mentioned in Psalm 6?

This, then, is what we learn from this Psalm; 1) you can have a genuine heart for the Lord, 2) and still grievously sin.

The major lesson from Psalm 6 is even when we willfully sin God's forgiveness, mercy, and restoration are still available! David was restored because of God's mercy. That same mercy and restoration is available to you, regardless of what you have done!

Biblical Thinking

Even when you are guilty of sin and the cause of the trial you are currently in God's grace and mercy are still available to you. Just ask Him! Trust God no matter what!

Chapter 17

What If I'm Innocent?

Psalm 7

What if you are the recipient of wrong doing, slandered, or betrayed by someone close to you? If so, then this Psalm is for you.

David was being persecuted and lies about him were being spread. He asked God for deliverance based on the grounds that he was innocent of what his enemies were saying about him. He wanted God to vindicate him by judging those against him. David declared that "My defense is of God," verse 10.

O Lord my God, in You I put my trust; Save me from all those who persecute me; And deliver me, 2 Lest they tear me like a lion, Rending me in pieces, while there is none to deliver.

3 O Lord my God, if I have done this: If there is iniquity in my hands, 4 If I have repaid evil to him who was at peace with me, Or have plundered my enemy without cause, 5 Let the enemy pursue me and overtake me; Yes, let him trample my life to the earth, And lay my honor in the dust. Selah

6 Arise, O Lord, in Your anger; Lift Yourself up because of the rage of my enemies; Rise up for me to the judgment You have commanded! 7 So the congregation of the peoples shall surround You; For their sakes, therefore, return on high.

8 The Lord shall judge the peoples; Judge me, O Lord, according to my righteousness, And according to my integrity within me.

9 Oh, let the wickedness of the wicked come to an end, But establish the just; For the righteous God tests the hearts and minds. 10 My defense is of God, Who saves the upright in heart.

11 God is a just judge, And God is angry with the wicked every day. 12 If he does not turn back, He will sharpen His sword; He bends His bow and makes it ready. 13 He also prepares for Himself instruments of death; He makes His arrows into fiery shafts.

14 Behold, the wicked brings forth iniquity; Yes, he conceives trouble and brings forth falsehood. 15 He made a pit and dug it out, And has fallen into the ditch which he made. 16 His trouble shall return upon his own head, And his violent dealing shall come down on his own crown.

17 I will praise the Lord according to His righteousness, And will sing praise to the name of the Lord Most High.

David begins with affirming his trust in God, v.1, and asking Him to save him from the persecution, v.2. In verses 3-5 David says if I have done anyone wrong then let his enemy defeat him.

Therefore, absent of his guilt, David ask God to then judge his enemies, verses 6-9. David then makes an ageless statement in verse 10, *My defense is of God.* No greater defense can be declared! Guilty or innocent our only defense is from God!

David then states the wicked will be judged because of their own deeds, verses 14-16.

Biblical Thinking

God is your only defense no matter what is happening. Trust Him no matter what!

PART V

BUT WHAT IF GOD DOESEN'T?

Chapter 18

God's Grace Is Sufficient

II Corinthians 12:7-10

Paul's Thorn in The Flesh

And lest I should be exalted above measure by the abundance of the revelations, a thorn in the flesh was given to me, a messenger of Satan to buffet me, lest I be exalted above measure. 8 Concerning this thing I pleaded with the Lord three times that it might depart from me. 9 And He said to me, "My grace is sufficient for you, for My strength is made perfect in weakness." Therefore most gladly I will rather boast in my infirmities, that the power of Christ may rest upon me. 10 Therefore I take pleasure in infirmities, in reproaches, in needs, in persecutions, in distresses, for Christ's sake. For when I am weak, then I am strong.

What if God doesn't respond to my plea for help when I need it the most? Sometimes He says "No" to our request. Paul had a thorn in the flesh and God refused to remove it. There has been much discussion about just what the "thorn" was but there is no clear answer. Dr. Tom Constable in his published notes on II Corinthians stated the following about Paul's thorn in the flesh:

Paul regarded his thorn in the flesh as a messenger that came from Satan to frustrate him (cf. Job 2:1-10). Nevertheless God had permitted it and would use it to bring good out of evil (Rom. 8:28).

It's clear that the reason God did not remove the thorn was to keep Paul humble. Paul stressed humility when he wrote the following in Romans 12:3...

> *For I say, through the grace given to me, to everyone who is among you, **not to think of himself more highly than he ought to think**, but to think soberly, as God has dealt to each one a measure of faith.*

What can we learn? Sometimes God allows things in our life to keep us humble and to show us that His grace is sufficient to get us through the most difficult situation, verse 9...

> *My grace is sufficient for you, for My strength is made perfect in weakness.*

If God does not work in your trial the way you want Him to just remember, His grace is there for you. He will be there for you and with you no matter what the outcome. Remember, that He promised to never leave you or forsake you, Hebrews 13:5-6...

> *Let your conduct be without covetousness; be content with such things as you have. For He Himself has said, "I will never leave you nor forsake you." 6 So we may boldly say: The Lord is my helper; I will not fear. What can man do to me?"*

Biblical Thinking

God's grace is sufficient no matter what happens. Trust God no matter what!

Chapter 19

Lessons From The Book of Job

Job 13:15

Though He slay me yet will I trust Him.

Job, some believe, may be the earilest book written in the Old Testament. The events and the writing of Job took place around 2,000 years before Christ was here so Job lived about 4,000 years ago.

Job was a very wealthy man and was an example of a Godly person (Job 1:8). Wealth was basically measured by the amount of children one had and the number of livestock owned.

In Job 1:1-12 God allowed Satan to try to get Job to denounse Him by taking everyhing he had. God said Job would not turn his back on Him regardless of what he lost.

In Job 1:13-19 four servents came to Job one right after the other to tell him he had lost all of his livestock, most of his servants, and his ten children. Job's response is in Job 1:21:

The Lord gave, and the Lord has taken away;
Blessed be the name of the Lord.

Next, Satan was given permission to attack Job physically as recorded in Job 2:6-8:

And the Lord said to Satan, "Behold, he is in your hand, but spare his life." 7 So Satan went out from the presence of the Lord, and struck Job with painful boils from the sole of his foot to the crown of his head. 8 And he took for himself a potsherd with which to scrape himself while he sat in the midst of the ashes.

This was too much for Job's wife! She threw her hands up and encouraged him to die, Job 2:9...

Then his wife said to him, "Do you still hold fast to your integrity? Curse God and die!"

Job did not flinch, he was not going to give in to the pressure that surrounded him. His answer to her demand is in Job 2:10...

But he said to her, "You speak as one of the foolish women speaks. Shall we indeed accept good from God, and shall we not accept adversity?"

Job's wife's response spotlights what many of us do. We praise God for His blessings but fail to see that God is still working when adversity strikes.

Two lessons. 1) The Lord gives and takes away. In either case God is worthy of praise. 2) We accept when God gives blessings and we should accept adversity. Job's response to what God was doing is seen in the following stages:

1. Initial Acceptance. When Job loses everything, he responds with humility and worship. This is what he lost: (Job 1-2):

- •Wealth and possessions
- •7,000 sheep
- •3,000 camels
- •500 yoke of oxen
- •500 female donkeys
- •Most servants killed
- •Ten children died
- •His health (sores & boils)
- •Social standing and comfort
- •Became an outcast
- •Friends turned on him

Again, this is Job's response (Job 1:21):

> *The LORD gave, and the LORD has taken away;*
> *blessed be the name of the LORD.*

He is devastated but he does not accuse God of wrongdoing.

2. Lament and questioning. As his suffering increases, Job becomes honest, he...

- •Laments his birth (Job 3).
- •Questions why God allows the righteous to suffer.
- •Defends his integrity and insists he does not deserved this suffering.

Note: Job questions God but he directs his complaints to God rather than complaining to others.

3. Encounter with God. When God finally speaks (Job 38–41), He does not explain the reasons for Job's suffering. Instead, He reveals His wisdom, power, and sovereignty over all of creation.

4. Humility and repentance. Job's final response is humility and submission, Job 42:3-6:

> *Surely I spoke of things I did not understand...*
> *Therefore I repent in dust and ashes.*

Job admits what we all need to accept; God's greatness and our own limited understanding of Who He is.

5. Restoration. God gave back to Job more than what was takened from him (Job 42):

- His physical health is restored.
- Wealth was doubled
- 14,000 sheep
- 6,000 camels
- 1,000 yoke of oxen
- 1,000 female donkeys
- Ten more children (7 boys & 3 girls)
- Long life and honor
- Lives 140 more years
- Sees four generations
- Dies "old and full of days"

Summary: The message of the book of Job by G. Michael Cocoris in *The Books of The Bible*, 2023, page 37 is "The overall message of Job is that a sovereign, wise God allows the righteous to suffer, not to punish them but to purify and perfect them."

Job's response in the book moves from: Trust → Struggle → Humility → Restoration.

He never fully understands why God allowed his suffering, but he comes to trust who God is; Job 13:15 *Though He slay me, yet will I trust Him.* The phrase expresses absolute trust in God, even in extreme suffering. Job declares that even if God allows me to suffer or die, I will still trust Him. We are to trust God not because life is good, but when life feels unbearable.

Job questions God and expresses his pain, yet he still chooses to trust Him. Faith doesn't depend on explanations or outcomes. Faith trusts God no matter what.

Biblical Thinking

Job is an incredible example. Trust God no matter what!

Chapter 20

God Is Able To Help You

John 1:1-5

In the beginning was the Word, and the Word was with God, and the Word was God. 2 He was in the beginning with God. 3 All things were made through Him, and without Him nothing was made that was made. 4 In Him was life, and the life was the light of men. 5 And the light shines in the darkness, and the darkness did not comprehend it.

When life's trouble storm into your life it is easy to forget just Who God is and the power He possesses. It is helpful to be reminded of God's incomprehensible power.

God is able to do anything

First, as recorded in John 1:1-5, God created all things. He did it by simply saying "Let it be..." as repeated in the first two chapters of Genesis many times. He just *spoke* and it was so! When the time came to create man He did so by borrowing from the ground. In Genesis 2:7 it is recorded that God used the *dust* of the ground to *shape* or *form* a man and then breathed into his nostrils and the form became a living soul. This means that God's breath alone created all the internal working parts of a human being.

93

Genesis 1:16. It's noteworthy that He used one word to create all the stars, *Then God made two great lights: the greater light to rule the day, and the lesser light to rule the night. He made the* **stars** *also.*

The Hebrew word for stars (kokab) is translated with just the one word. Think about that. So powerful is God that with one word He created innumerable stars. So massive that the deeper we look into the known universe the more stars we see. Scientist have suggested that there are approximately 200 billion trillion stars in the universe. Probably that number is not even close.

The size of the universe is also incompressible. For example, light travels around 5.88 trillion miles in one year and the farthest galaxy is 32 billion light years away! We can say with the Psalmist, *Such knowledge is too wonderful for me; it is high, I cannot attain unto it,* (Ps. 139:6).

What's the point? God did all of this with speaking and we worry about our current situation? Why?

The resurrection of Jesus
God is so powerful that even death cannot stop His will from being accomplished. Jesus was crucified for our sins and three days later He was raised from the dead, Luke 24:6-7...

> *He is not here, but is risen! Remember how He spoke to you when He was still in Galilee, 7 saying, "The Son of Man must be delivered into the hands of sinful men, and be crucified, and the third day rise again."*

God parted the Red Sea

You remember the story (Exodus 24) when Israel left Egypt under the leadership of Moses. When Pharaoh found out he became angry and sent his army after them. When all seemed lost for the children of Israel, when it appeared there was no reason to have hope, and when death seemed imminent, God took over! They were trapped with the Red Sea in front of them and the army of Pharaoh behind them. The children of Israel were exceedingly afraid and cried out for help from the Lord and then turned on Moses. They said it would have been better to have stayed in Egypt than to die in the wilderness. Here is what Moses told them, Exodus 24:13-14...

> *And Moses said to the people, "Do not be afraid. Stand still, and see the salvation of the Lord, which He will accomplish for you today. For the Egyptians whom you see today, you shall see again no more forever. 14 The Lord will fight for you, and you shall hold your peace."*

The Red sea was parted so that the children of Israel walked over on dry land (not mud)! Pharaoh's army tried to follow but the Red Sea collapsed killing them all.

What's the point? When things seem impossible trust God, when your back is to the wall, trust God! God created all things, He raised Jesus from the dead, and He parted the Red Sea, and we worry? Why?

Remember, God can do anything:

> He put a baby is Sarah's arms.
> He parted the Red Sea for Israel.
> He closed the lions mouth for Daniel.
> He stopped the sun for Joshua.
> He healed a blind man.
> He raised Lazarus from the dead.
> He opened the prison for Peter.

Biblical Thinking

God is capable of doing anything. He can help you in your current situation, so trust Him no matter what!

Chapter 21

God Is Willing To Help You

The Bible clearly teaches that God is not only willing to help you, He is eager! He is a compassionate, faithful Father who responds to those who trust Him.

God's willingness is rooted in His character of love, grace, mercy, and faithfulness. God understands and wants to give you peace when you trust Him. Here are a few passages that show God's willingness to help you:

1. **Hebrews 13:6** God is described as a source of help for those who trust Him. The writer of Hebrews is actually quoting from Palm 118.

> *So we may boldly say: "The Lord is my helper;*
> *I will not fear. What can man do to me?*

2. **Psalm 46:1-2** God is ready and willing to help His people when they call on Him:

> *God is our refuge and strength,*
> *A very present help in trouble.*
> *2 Therefore we will not fear,*

Isaiah 41:10

Fear not, for I am with you;
Be not dismayed, for I am your God.
I will strengthen you, Yes, I will help you,
I will uphold you with My righteous right hand.

3. **Luke 11:9-10** God encourages us to *ask* with the promise that God will respond.

Ask, and it will be given...
for everyone who asks receives.

4. **James 1:5** Ask God if you do not understand your trial. He gives generously and without reproach.

If any of you lacks wisdom, let him ask of God,
who gives to all liberally and without reproach,
and it will be given to him.

5. **1 Corinthians 10:13** God helps you in times of trial and temptation. Paul wrote that God never abandons believers to overwhelming temptation, but provides a way out and enables endurance.

No temptation has overtaken you except such as is common to man; but God is faithful, who will not allow you to be tempted beyond what you are able, but with the temptation will also make the way of escape, that you may be able to bear it.

Old Testament Verses

Psalm 46:1 *God is our refuge and strength, an ever-present help in trouble.*

Psalm 28:7 *The Lord is my strength and my shield; my heart trusted in Him, and I am helped.*

Psalm 34:17 *The righteous cry out, and the Lord hears and delivers them out of all their troubles.*

Psalm 118:6-7 – "The Lord is on my side… the Lord helped me."

Nahum 1:7 *The Lord is good, a stronghold in the day of trouble; and He knows those who trust in Him.*

Psalm 37:5 *Commit your way to the Lord; trust in Him, and He will act.*

New Testament Verses

Hebrews 4:16 *Let us…approach God's throne of grace…that we may receive mercy and find grace to help in time of need.*

Hebrews 13:6 *The Lord is my helper; I will not be afraid.*

1 Peter 5:7 *Cast all your anxieties on Him, because He cares for you.*

Psalm 55:22 *Cast your burden on the Lord, and He will sustain you.*

Summary: God is eager to respond to your need. He wants you to ask and trust Him (no matter what) for an answer. He responds to those who ask.

Chapter 22

Impossible Situation?

II Corithians 1:8-9

Paul Was Completely Overwhelmed

*We do not want you to be uninformed, brothers and sisters, about the troubles we experienced in the province of Asia. We were under great pressure, far beyond our ability to endure, so that we despaired of life itself. 9 Indeed, we felt we had received the sentence of death. **But this happened that we might not rely on ourselves but on God, who raises the dead**.*

When Paul wrote this letter to the believers in Corinth he had experienced such trouble that he believed that his life was over! We do not know for sure what had happened but we do know he thought it was a death sentence (1:9).

Yes, even the Apostle Paul experienced such impossible odds that he *despaired* of life itself. The word *despaired* means "to be utterly at a loss, to renounce all hope." It appears that the believers in Corinth did not understand the intense emotions that Paul had felt.

Do you feel the situation you are in has removed all hope that it will be resolved in your favor? Do you feel it is impossible? If this is where you are right now, keep reading.

Notice what Paul writes next, *But this happened that we might not rely on ourselves*. God allowed the situation to be so overwhelming that there was absolutely nothing Paul could do to get out of his circumstance. It's implied that Paul did everything he could do and it had failed. He was completely hopeless!

Paul then adds, *but God*! Paul was not to rely on himself to get out of the situation but to trust God. What follows is the reason Paul should rely on God, *who raises the dead*! Paul asserts that there is no reason for him to be concerned because God is so powerful that He can raise the dead!

Whatever you are facing, no matter how impossible it looks, remember the power of God, He can raise the dead! Why then should you worry? Trust God to resolve your situation. Paul did and he was delivered, *He has delivered us from such a deadly peril, and he will deliver us again* (II Corinthians 1:10.

Biblical Thinking

Since God is capable of raising the dead, He can do anything. He can help you in your current situation so trust Him no matter what!

Chapter 23

Wait On God

Proverbs 20:22

Do not say, "I will recompense evil";
Wait for the Lord, and He will save you.

Waiting on the Lord to do something is as difficult a task as any. A trial can last a few hours, days, months or even years. Whether short or long many times God asks us to wait on Him to do something.

The proverb opens by instructing us to not *reciprocate* the evil done to you. Romans 12:17-19 says that is God's job.

Repay no one evil for evil. Have regard for good things in the sight of all men. 18 If it is possible, as much as depends on you, live peaceably with all men. 19 Beloved, do not avenge yourselves, but rather give place to wrath; for it is written, "Vengeance is Mine, I will repay," says the Lord.

The word "wait' in Proverb 20:22 holds the idea to *wait with hope and expectation*. So we are not to just sit back by with no hope. The opposite is true, we are to wait expecting God to do something in our favor.

The following poem is by Deborah Ann Belka:

103

Today I sent to God,
a S.O.S . . .
He replied back to me
My child don't you stress.

He told me He was working,
on an answer to my prayer
until then I was to relax
and not fall into despair.

I asked Him how long,
He was going to take
He said it would be soon
His decision He would make.

So I took His advice,
and rested in His care
knowing His response
was somewhere out there.

Today I sent to God,
a S.O.S . . .
He signaled back to me
into Him to deeper press!

Bibical Thinking

It pleases God when you wait on Him to do something. Trust God no matter what!

Chapter 24

How Should I Pray?

1 John 5:14

*And this is the confidence that we have in him, that, if we ask any thing **according to his will**, he heareth us:*

First, we are to pray according to His will as stated in I John 5:14 above. James 4:15 states, *Instead you ought to say, "**If the Lord wills**, we shall live and do this or that.* Jesus said in Matthew 6:10, *Your kingdom come. **Your will be done** On earth as it is in heaven.*

When you pray always end with asking God to have His will in your situation. Then, *Let us therefore come boldly to the throne of grace, that we may obtain mercy and find grace to help in time of need,* Hebrews 4:16. Whatever your circumstance, you can ask God for mercy and grace. You can ask for wisdom if do not fully understand how to handle the trial correctly. You should keep on asking God to work on your behalf until He does.

When you leave the results of your situation up to God, He will give you peace, Philippians 4:6-7.

Biblical Thinking
Ask God for anything and trust Him for His will to be done.

Chapter 25

Be Content

Philippians 4:11–13

Not that I speak in regard to need, for I have learned in whatever state I am, to be content: 12 I know how to [a]be abased, and I know how to [b]abound. Everywhere and in all things I have learned both to be full and to be hungry, both to abound and to suffer need. 13 I can do all things through [c]Christ who strengthens me.

Contentment is the result of trusting God no matter what. It is described in the Bible as a state of being satisfied and at peace with what you have.

Being content is not dependent on external possessions or circumstances but is rooted in a deep trust in God's provision and sovereignty. The Apostle Paul exemplifies this attitude, stating that he has learned to be content in all situations, emphasizing that true strength comes from trusting God for what He is doing in your life.

By trusting God no matter what you can cultivate a heart of contentment, recognizing that your fulfillment in life does not come from circumstances but from your relationship with Him.

My brother, Mike (pastor in California, at age 71), in 2011 had a life changing experience. An abscess soddenly wrapped around his spinal cord causing him to loose nearly all feelings from his waist down. He was paralyzed! The doctors told him that he would never walk again!

I was counseling a neurosurgeon at the time and explained the situation to him to get his opinion. He confirmed that spinal cord injuries are "unforgiving" and that he most likely would never walk again.

My wife and I flew out to California to see him. I asked him, "how are you doing ... really?" He responded, "It has not occurred to me to be upset, the Lord gives and the Lord takes away, blessed be the name of the Lord." Mike's wife, Patricia, recently said to his congregation that, "I've never heard him complain one time."

My brother has trusted God no matter what was going on all of his christian life. He learned to accept whatever God was doing in his life all of his life.

Mike is now 86 and is able to walk! Mike sometimes uses a cain but basically walks on his own. He took a group to Israel six years ago (my wife and I were in the group). He went back at 86!

Biblical Thinking
Contement comes from trusting God no matter what!

Chapter 26

Conclusion

When you are suddenly surrounded by life's trials remember to not be surprised. Trials are God's chosen method to help you become conformed into the image of Christ. Remember that God doesn't do anything *to* you, He allows it *for* you.

Your thinking needs to align with what the Bible teaches. It's not enough to *know* what God said, you have to actually *do* what God has said.

You are to have *calm delight* in a trial because God is at work to bring you to spiritual maturity. You are not to get anxious, angry, or depressed over what is happening in your life.

Trust God no matter what. God has opened the door for you to approach the Throne of Grace to ask for mercy and grace no matter what has happened or what you have done. He has promised to never leave you or forsake you.

If you don't understand what is happening you can ask God to give you wisdom and understanding. You have been given permission to keep on asking for Him to work in your situation whether you've caused the situation or not.

If things do not turn out in your favor God's grace is sufficient to get you through the situation. God is capable of working in an impossible situation. Trust God no matter what!

Noah's Ark

On the cover of this book is a picture of Noah's ark. It shows the rain was just beginning to fall and the ark was already sealed with God's chosen passengers. Soon the whole world would be covered with water; Genesis 6:9-22 (full story in chapters 7-9). It's quite the understatement to say that Noah needed to trust God no matter what was happening!

God gave Noah specific instructions on how to build the ark. But the instructions did not include a rudder! How did God expect Noah to steer the boat without a rudder?

Well, God never intended for Noah to be the captain and steer the boat. The Ark was designed for floating only.

God was the Captain and He was in charge of protecting the passengers and directing the boat!

Lesson? The absence of a rudder symbolizes complete trust in God to steer the boat. Let God steer you through whatever you're going through. Trust God no matter what! He knows what He is doing.

Appendix

When In The Trial Quote Scripture

Going through a trial can cause many different and conflicting thoughts and emotions. They often come fast and furious leaving you numb searching for peace.

Unchecked, these thoughts and feelings will distract you from growing spiritually by keeping your focus on the problem instead of on God.

To defeat a negative thought or feeling quote a passage or part of a passage *as soon as you are aware* that you are having a negative moment. The Bible is full of verses to remember at such a time. Here are a few from this book:

1. When asking why - Quote **Romans 8:28**

   All things work together for good..

2. When angry - Quote *Ephesians 4:32*

   Be angry and sin not, let not the sun
   go down on your wrath.

3. When anxious - Quote **Philippians 4:5**

   Be anxious for nothing...

4. When doubting - Quote **Proverbs 3:5-6**

   Trust in the Lord with all your heart, And lean not
   on your own understanding; 6 In all your ways
   acknowledge Him, And He shall direct your paths.

5. When unforgiving - Quote **Ephesians 4:26**

    *Be kind to one another, tenderhearted,
    forgiving one another, as God in Christ
    forgave you.*

6. When desperate - Quote **Hebrews 4:16**

    *Let us therefore come boldly to the throne
    of grace, that we may obtain mercy and
    find grace to help in time of need.*

7. When confused - Quote **James 1:5**

    *If any of you lacks wisdom, let him ask of
    God, who gives to all liberally and without
    reproach, and it will be given to him.*

8. When heavy hearted - Quote **Luke 18:7**

    *And shall God not avenge His own elect
    who cry out day and night to Him.*

9. When guilty - *Quote* **Psalm 6:2**

    Have mercy on me, O Lord, for I am weak;

10. When God says no - *Quote **II Corinthians 12:9***

    *My grace is sufficient for you, for My strength
    is made perfect in weakness.*

11. When facing an impossible situation:

Quote **II Cor 1:9**

But this happened that we might not rely on ourselves but on God, who raises the dead.

Quote **Psalm 7:10**

My defense is of God.

My wife had to learn a new way to make a deposit at our bank. New technology replaced the typical clerk behind the counter and replaced her with an ATM machine.

At first it was challenging to figure out the new steps to complete a deposit. She had to ask for help several times before learning the new approach. She said to me "It is easy now that I figured it out!"

If you practice what God has said about nagivating trials, and getting some help, you too will say, "It's easy now that I've figured it out!"

Trust God no matter what!

Check List

How Am I Doing?

☐ I will not be surprised when trials rush into my life.

☐ I believe that *all things* work together for good.

☐ I will think Biblically.

☐ I will do what God says.

☐ I want *calm delight* in a trial.

☐ I will not get *angry* in a trial.

☐ I will not get *anxious* in a trial.

☐ I will not *fear* in a trial.

☐ I will not get *depressed* in a trial.

☐ I will *trust* God no matter what happens.

☐ I will *forgive* those that have harmed me.

☐ I will *come boldly* to the Throne of Grace.

☐ I will ask for *wisdom* on how to respond to my trisl.

☐ I will *not stop asking* God for help.

☐ I will ask for God's *mercy* even if I'm guilty.

☐ I will ask God for *justice* if I'm innocent.

☐ I believe that God's *grace is sufficient.*

☐ I believe God is *capable.*

☐ I believe God is *willing.*

☐ I will *wait* on God to work.

☐ I will pray asking for *God's will* to be done.

☐ I will *trust God* no matter what!

About The Author

John T. Cocoris has devoted his life since 1977 to develop and promote the temperament model of behavior. John has a B.A. from Tennessee Temple University, a Masters of Theology (Th. M.) from Dallas Theological Seminary, a Masters in Counseling (M.A.) from Amberton University, and a Doctorate in Psychology (Psy.D.) from California Coast University. John was a licensed therapist in the state of Texas from 1995-2020.

John established Profile Dynamics in the early 1980's to develop the temperament model of behavior for use in business and counseling. He has been a management consultant since 1984 and has worked with a variety of companies giving seminars for training managers and sales people.

John has conducted seminars in churches to help church counselors help others. John has also trained other therapists in the use of the temperament model in counseling. John has been interviewed on the radio and has been featured numerous times on COPE, a national cable TV talk show.

John and Phillip Moss formed Temperament Dynamics, LLC in 2017 to further develop, expand, and promote the temperament model of behavior.

John has written several books and manuals: *Why We Do What We Do, New Insights Into The Temperament Model of Behavior; Born With A Creative Temperament, The Sanguine-Melancholy (I-C); 7 Steps To A Better You, How To Develop Your Natural Tendencies; A Parent's Guide To Helping Your Child Develop Their Natural Temperament Tendencies; A Leader's Guide To Using The Temperament Model of Behavior; How To Sell Using The Temperament Model of Behavior; Man's Wisdom or God's Wisdom, Trust God No Matter What!*; The DISC II Temperament Assessment; The DISC3 Temperament Assessment; The Temperament Profile Assessment, and The Temperament Profile Assessment User's Guide.

www.ingramcontent.com/pod-product-compliance
Lightning Source LLC
Chambersburg PA
CBHW060243030426
42335CB00014B/1577